# THE WORLD IN MY WORDS

Edited By Jenni Harrison

First published in Great Britain in 2024 by:

Young Writers
Remus House
Coltsfoot Drive
Peterborough
PE2 9BF
Telephone: 01733 890066
Website: www.youngwriters.co.uk

All Rights Reserved
Book Design by Ashley Janson
© Copyright Contributors 2023
Softback ISBN 978-1-83565-134-6

Printed and bound in the UK by BookPrintingUK
Website: www.bookprintinguk.com
YB0577Q

# FOREWORD

For Young Writers' latest competition This Is Me, we asked primary school pupils to look inside themselves, to think about what makes them unique, and then write a poem about it! They rose to the challenge magnificently and the result is this fantastic collection of poems in a variety of poetic styles.

Here at Young Writers our aim is to encourage creativity in children and to inspire a love of the written word, so it's great to get such an amazing response, with some absolutely fantastic poems. It's important for children to focus on and celebrate themselves and this competition allowed them to write freely and honestly, celebrating what makes them great, expressing their hopes and fears, or simply writing about their favourite things. This Is Me gave them the power of words. The result is a collection of inspirational and moving poems that also showcase their creativity and writing ability.

I'd like to congratulate all the young poets in this anthology, I hope this inspires them to continue with their creative writing.

# CONTENTS

**Independent Entrants**

Isabelle Smith-Strachan — 1

**Buckingham Park CE Primary School, Buckingham Park**

Reema Gundu (8) — 2
Tiara Khara (8) — 3
Robin Brar (8) — 4
Jadiell Ajantharuban (8) — 5
Alicia Chikwanha (8) — 6
Matilda Keith (8) — 7
Jack Allum (8) — 8
Nila Krishna (8) — 9
Lucy Driscoll (8) — 10
Annabel Norris (8) — 11
Hayley Edwards (8) — 12
Jordan Cheung (8) — 13
Beau Bradley (8) — 14
Tessnim Laghdas (8) — 15
Libby Brandon (8) — 16
Lillie Davies (8) — 17
Ethan Webb (8) — 18
Mary-Jane Nevin (8) — 19
Aida Pennicott (8) — 20
Polly Lofting (8) — 21
Sofia Suman (8) — 22
Evelyn Ni (8) — 23
Conan Bennison (8) — 24
Louis Gordon (8) — 25
Oliver Gordon (8) — 26
Roman Wilson (8) — 27
Ruha Nattar (9) — 28
Musa Ahmed (8) — 29
Katie Knight-Whiddett (8) — 30

**Raynham Primary School, Edmonton**

Izabela Roszyk (10) — 31
Aylin Ciledag (11) — 32
Sarah Le — 34
Eiliah Homar (9) — 36
Alicja Werner (7) — 37
Lewan Bakr (9) — 38
Eyasu Tesfaldet (11) — 39
Aaminah Surti (7) — 40

**St Bartholomew's CE Primary School, Stourport-On-Severn**

Joseph Sutton (9) — 41
Toby Woodhouse (9) — 42
Herbie Nunn (9) — 43
Olivia Augyte (10) — 44
Caelum Hill (10) — 45
Blake Thomas (9) — 46
Corey James Clark (9) — 47
Cowen Ash (9) — 48

**St Edward's Royal Free Ecumenical Middle School, Windsor**

Eliana Kozliar (10) — 49
Alice — 50

**St George's School, Edgbaston**

Ernest Punkenhofer-Silve (8) — 52
Emma Szlanka (7) — 54
Abdullah Araf (8) — 55
Karanveer — 56

| | |
|---|---|
| Jode Lotay | 57 |
| Mukul Kottilil (8) | 58 |
| Alicia Roberts (9) | 59 |
| Mikail Iqbal (8) | 60 |
| Kasim Iqbal (7) | 61 |
| Buhari | 62 |

## St Hugh's CE Primary School, Holts

| | |
|---|---|
| Carolina Malpao (9) | 63 |
| Josie-Lea Seddon (8) | 64 |
| Casper Marczynski (8) | 65 |
| Fariyah Farooq (8) | 66 |
| Macie-Dee Seddon (8) | 67 |
| Christopher Allen (9) | 68 |
| Kyron Peers (9) | 69 |
| Reis Matoshi (9) | 70 |
| Ellis Musoni (8) | 71 |
| Abigail Aina (8) | 72 |
| Lexi Taylor (9) | 73 |
| Mika Ross (9) | 74 |
| Byron Pember (8) | 75 |
| Jakub Gryszka (9) | 76 |
| Daniel Allen (8) | 77 |
| Naomi Kendra Ndlovu (8) | 78 |

## St Mary's Primary School Dunsford, Ardglass

| | |
|---|---|
| Keeva Gilchrist (11) | 79 |
| Eva Mae Magee (8) | 80 |
| Isabelle Burns (10) | 81 |
| Nicole Karbauske (8) | 82 |
| Lottie Smyth (8) | 83 |
| David Kelly (10) | 84 |
| Harry Gilchrist (9) | 85 |
| Ollie Mc Mullan (9) | 86 |
| Rossa Curran (8) | 87 |
| Dara Gilchrist (8) | 88 |
| Callum Moreland (9) | 89 |
| Michelle Sniuke (8) | 90 |
| Callum Mc Ilmail (9) | 91 |

## St Michael's RC Primary School, East Ham

| | |
|---|---|
| Jack Bell (6) | 92 |
| Nohan Jose (6) | 93 |
| Cruz Vickery (6) | 94 |
| Stephanie Bartha (6) | 95 |
| Mayan Fagan (6) | 96 |
| Szofi Gal (6) | 97 |
| Janella Budu-Aggrey (6) | 98 |
| Ayva-Oakly Annan-Mathieu (6) | 99 |
| Skylar Delisser (7) | 100 |
| Elkhanah Theresa Shijanjose (6) | 101 |
| Anaiah Grace Oduwole (7) | 102 |
| Ishmael Menchaca (6) | 103 |
| Evaan Joharsingh (6) | 104 |
| Joseph Ogarro (7) | 105 |
| River Carter (6) | 106 |
| Stacey Wu (7) | 107 |
| Sarthak Pathak (6) | 108 |
| Riya Jerry (6) | 109 |
| Nadal Maxwell (6) | 110 |
| Natchatrah Sivamathan | 111 |
| Anastasia Berdaga-Roabis (6) | 112 |
| Isaac Wilson (7) | 113 |
| Neymar Maxwell (6) | 114 |
| Poppy O'Connell (6) | 115 |
| Cianna Green | 116 |

## Stonesfield Primary School, Stonesfield

| | |
|---|---|
| Rocco Hulcup (11) | 117 |
| Freya Harris (10) | 118 |
| James Hunt (10) | 119 |
| Isaac Smyth-Medina (11) | 120 |
| Abel Stuart (10) | 121 |
| Leland Edwards (10) | 122 |

# THE POEMS

# This Is Me

This is me
My name is Isabelle, and you are going to discover more about me.
My favourite colour is galaxy because it makes me feel happy.
I love my family and I love puppies and I'm not bossy.
My name is Isabelle, not Isabella, as my name ends with an E, not an A.
Funny is my smile as I enjoy laughter.
Happiness is a flower in spring, and I am a flower.
My name is Isabelle and I love me.

**Isabelle Smith-Strachan**

# This Is Me!

Welcome, welcome - this is me!
Come take a seat for a cup of masala tea,
Let's talk, let's chat all about... ME!

I'm literally obsessed with sunshine-yellow,
However since I was little I've always hated marshmallow.
"This is me," declares the rising sun.

I'm a monkey, however I cannot yet climb trees, also I hate to eat peas.
"This is me," hiding beneath the shadows.

I'm as intelligent as a gorilla, however I'm not so smart to get a free private villa.
"This is me," a melody through space and time.

I am as flexible as a perfect pretzel, on the other hand, my writing with a pencil is exactly like a pretzel with lots of twists and turns.
"This is me," as the heart sings.

I am unique, not a copy or a mirrored reflection.
Guess what I am, "This is me."

**Reema Gundu (8)**
Buckingham Park CE Primary School, Buckingham Park

# This Is Me!

**T** errific as a tiger
**I** ncredible as a dolphin
**A** mazing as a monkey
**R** idiculous as a clown
**A** stonishing as an eagle

**K** ind like a butterfly
**H** opeful like a star
**A** monkey like my sister
**R** oblox is fun like colouring
**A** n artist like my mummy.

**Tiara Khara (8)**
Buckingham Park CE Primary School, Buckingham Park

# This Is Me!

I like ice cream
I like money
I am funny
I like monkeys
This is me!
You can't change me
I will be me
I love me
This is me
You can't change me
This is me
You can't change me
I'm as funny as a penguin and I know who I am
This is meeeeeeeeee!

**Robin Brar (8)**
Buckingham Park CE Primary School, Buckingham Park

# This Is Me And My Life

This is me and my life
Hi, this is me, come read this poem with a cup of sweet tea!
Whenever I am in a swimming pool people say I am not cool!
My sister is a blister!
When I read a book my mum tells me to cook!
As I chew bubblegum, I always say yum yum!
I love sweets and sweets love me!

### Jadiell Ajantharuban (8)
Buckingham Park CE Primary School, Buckingham Park

# This Is Me

**A** mazing
**L** earn
**I** ntelligent
**C** alm
**I** mpressive
**A** mbition

**C** ares
**H** opes
**I** nspires
**K** ind
**W** ow
**A** rranges games
**N** ice
**H** appy
**A** wesome.

## Alicia Chikwanha (8)
Buckingham Park CE Primary School, Buckingham Park

# This Is Me - Who I'll Always Be

M acarons are mine
A mazing as an antelope
T rick or treat is so yummy
I ce tea sounds nice
L azy life on the weekend
D escendants and zombies are dancing movies
A xolotls are cute, and pet ones are better.

**Matilda Keith (8)**
Buckingham Park CE Primary School, Buckingham Park

# This Is Me!

J olly is me
A ntonov 225 is my favourite plane
C aring I am
K ind also

A lso, I
L ove my mum
L ove my dad
U tterly love walking
M &M's are my favourite.

## Jack Allum (8)
Buckingham Park CE Primary School, Buckingham Park

# This Is Me!

I love books and I have glasses to help me look.
I love to dance but I'm pretty calm so I'd rather not prance.
I'm shy however I don't like to cry.
Part of me is I love turquoise and tea.
I love dogs and dogs love me!

## Nila Krishna (8)
Buckingham Park CE Primary School, Buckingham Park

# To Make Me...

To make me:
Add a hand full of horse
Add art
Blend black
Measure my dog
Carve calm
Squeeze quiet into a bowl
Decorate kind then drizzle on my dog
Blend books
Bake in the oven then serve a slice.

**Lucy Driscoll (8)**
Buckingham Park CE Primary School, Buckingham Park

# To Make Me...

To make me:
Add a dollop of sloth.
Stir in a spoonful of silly.
Shake well with purple.
Mix with some funny.
Add a bit of Roblox,
A handful of Harry Potter.
Bake in the oven and
This is me.

**Annabel Norris (8)**
Buckingham Park CE Primary School, Buckingham Park

# This Is Me

**H** onest to everyone
**A** mazing friends that help
**Y** ouTuber - I make videos
**L** ovely to everyone
**E** xtremely kind to everyone
**Y** oung and kind - to young and old.

**Hayley Edwards (8)**
Buckingham Park CE Primary School, Buckingham Park

# This Is Me

**J** umpy like a kangaroo
**O** verjoyed like an axolotl
**R** eally fast like a rhino
**D** ashing like a dolphin
**A** wesome like a roller coaster
**N** ever naughty.

**Jordan Cheung (8)**
Buckingham Park CE Primary School, Buckingham Park

# This Is Me

This is me, who I'll always be,
I'm mad about maths,
I love my family,
Pink and blue are my favourite colours
Because they make me me
Harry Potter is my cup of tea.

**Beau Bradley (8)**
Buckingham Park CE Primary School, Buckingham Park

# This Is Me

I am terrific as an artist.
I do exploring like an explorer.
I am like a sunset.
I am as sweet as a lollipop.
I am nice like a flower.
I am intelligent like a flash of IQ.

## Tessnim Laghdas (8)
Buckingham Park CE Primary School, Buckingham Park

# To Be Libby

Add a dollop of slime
A pinch of baby blue glitter
A drop of blue pigment
Add purple foam beads for extra crunch
Then stir it
It's not sticky - that's my recipe.

## Libby Brandon (8)
Buckingham Park CE Primary School, Buckingham Park

# This Is Me

Add a dollop of dogs
Stir in a spoonful of glitter
Shake well
Put code in
Mix with a sneaky doughnut
Put Stitch in and more dogs
Bake in the oven and this is me.

## Lillie Davies (8)
Buckingham Park CE Primary School, Buckingham Park

# This Is Me!

Stir a spoon of silliness
Fill in with mad footy
Millions in bags
Louder than a lion's roar
Add a bit of cheekiness
Bake it in the oven
Then - this is me.

**Ethan Webb (8)**
Buckingham Park CE Primary School, Buckingham Park

# This Is Me!

Mix with some rabbits
Add with some dogs
Mix some Roblox
Roblox is fun for me - it is fun for everyone
Add a swimming pool
Making cakes and doughnuts with my mom!

## Mary-Jane Nevin (8)
Buckingham Park CE Primary School, Buckingham Park

# To Make Me...

To make me
Toss in a handful of sparkly glitter
Add the drizzle of blue pompoms
Mash the green juicy pickle
Shake the funny well
Then give it to your dog first.

**Aida Pennicott (8)**
Buckingham Park CE Primary School, Buckingham Park

# This Is Me

I'm crazy and clever,
Love turquoise and dogs,
Add in Harry Potter,
And Prime and lime,
My sister is a blister,
Roblox is a blockster,
This is me.

## Polly Lofting (8)
Buckingham Park CE Primary School, Buckingham Park

# This Is Me!

I'm kind
I'm honest and caring
I'm amazing at drawing
How about you?
Are you amazing too?
I love my family
Without them, where would I be?

**Sofia Suman (8)**
Buckingham Park CE Primary School, Buckingham Park

# This Is Me!

**E** xcellent
**V** ictory
**E** xtra amazing
**L** ovely
**Y** oung
**N** onsense

**N** ice
**I** ntelligent.

## Evelyn Ni (8)
Buckingham Park CE Primary School, Buckingham Park

# This Is Me!

**C** razy for Minecraft.
**O** ver the top about YouTube.
**N** ever hates Minecraft.
**A** games warrior.
**N** ever hates football.

## Conan Bennison (8)
Buckingham Park CE Primary School, Buckingham Park

# This Is Me

**L** ego is fun
**O** verexcited as an ostrich
**U** nicycles are hard to ride
**I** am good at football
**S** mart at maths.

## Louis Gordon (8)
Buckingham Park CE Primary School, Buckingham Park

# This Is Me

Train lover, I go undercover
Do you like honey? Buy some money
Are you out of time? Buy some Prime
I'm an actor! Are you a raptor?

**Oliver Gordon (8)**
Buckingham Park CE Primary School, Buckingham Park

# This Is Me

**R** oblox man
**O** bsidian - I'm tough
**M** anly me
**A** mazing as an aardvark
**N** atty natterer.

## Roman Wilson (8)
Buckingham Park CE Primary School, Buckingham Park

# This Is Me!

Add a dollop of dinosaurs.
Bake some homemade brownies
Add my family
I love my family and my family love me.

**Ruha Nattar (9)**
Buckingham Park CE Primary School, Buckingham Park

# This Is Me

Add a slice of chocolate cake
Stir in FIFA mobile
Mix with a cheetah
Add golden cake
This is me.

## Musa Ahmed (8)
Buckingham Park CE Primary School, Buckingham Park

# This Is Me

**K** ind
**A** mazing
**T** errific
**I** ntelligent
**E** xcellent.

## Katie Knight-Whiddett (8)
Buckingham Park CE Primary School, Buckingham Park

# This Is Me

I'll let myself be confident,
Brave or strong.
Others may think I'm crazy,
But I think they're wrong.
I'll let myself know beauty,
And others may know my mind.
The cure to 'rude'
Is impossible to find.
When days feel like weeks,
It's honestly tough.
Sometimes,
People don't know what's enough.
But I'll be by your side,
No matter what
I'll stick up for you,
Stronger than super glue.
My voice will sing you a lullaby
Rock you to sleep.
I'll be with you along the way,
Just don't dig deep.

**Izabela Roszyk (10)**
Raynham Primary School, Edmonton

# This Is Me

Soon when you look up at the moon
You will be lost in thought
Wondering if anyone has ever belonged to the glowing moon
Well I do, Aylin does
Or maybe that's just what it means
It's a pretty distinctive name right?
I mean, I won't say I'm exactly perfect
My anger gets ahead of me sometimes
My doe eyes are a combination of gold, green and brown
My dirty blonde hair goes all over the place
And I'm often really messy when it comes to tidying up
When I start to feel distressed
I open my AirPods
And I feel this electric warmth
Music often feels like my escape from everything
My mysterious future has often been a dream
I'm just an average 11-year-old Turkish girl

But I'm a great listener
And I'll always be here to listen to you.

## Aylin Ciledag (11)
Raynham Primary School, Edmonton

# This Is Me

This is me!
My personality is kind
My personality is funny
My personality is smart
And I'm as happy as a bunny!

This is me!
I have a smart sister
And I have a big brother
I love my dad
And I love my mother

This is me!
I am from Vietnam
And I love my food
Such as pho
And I love some bun

This is me!
I love everything about me

I love my family
I am proud of myself
Because this is me!

## Sarah Le
Raynham Primary School, Edmonton

# My Place

M ango palm tree blooming their fruit
A mazing beaming sun outside
U ltra juicy mango drizzle
R acing up and down to find sugar around
I t is just like I have turned into a honey cloud
T oday, juicy mango, sweet bananas and cream with coconut
I t is a tropical island
U ntil you hear birds tweeting and cats meowing
S tay in Mauritius, beautiful puffy clouds, tropical fruit to find!

**Eiliah Homar (9)**
Raynham Primary School, Edmonton

# This Is Me

I am as smart as a fox
I am as sweet as honey
I am a funny person
Who likes dogs

Sometimes I am happy
Sometimes I am strong
Sometimes I am weak
Sometimes I am wrong

I might have plenty of money
I am beautiful or not
But I should be precious
As my thoughts.

## Alicja Werner (7)
Raynham Primary School, Edmonton

# This Is Me

My dad is Iraqi
We make Dolma at home
I am Iraqi
My mum is Turkish
We make Turkish tea
I am Turkish
My school is Raynham Primary School
We are multicultural
I am British
Different culture
Different dish
I am
Iraqi, Turkish and British
I am me!

**Lewan Bakr (9)**
Raynham Primary School, Edmonton

# This Is Me

**E** nergetic and enthusiastic like a cheetah
**Y** appy and young like a puppy
**A** ctive and adventurous, an anteater looking for food
**S** trong and smart, a body builder in a gym
**U** seful and unique, that's me!

## Eyasu Tesfaldet (11)
Raynham Primary School, Edmonton

# This Is Me

I'm as sweet as a flower
I have hidden power
I'm small and pretty
As cute as a kitty
I love to read
I take the lead
I swim like a fish
Chicken is my favourite dish
I'm full of happiness
This is me!

**Aaminah Surti (7)**
Raynham Primary School, Edmonton

# A Recipe

1st gather a pot of lightning energy
2nd stir in a book of love and tricks
3rd it's the season of love, why don't you come over here and give me a big hug?
4th spiralling happiness of rap
5th and a bucket of intelligence
6th pour in a tsunami of rap
7th slowly practise your rap skills during the weekends
8th when the fun doctor comes out to play
9th this is my favourite tortoise 'Tebby'.

**Joseph Sutton (9)**
St Bartholomew's CE Primary School, Stourport-On-Severn

# Excited

E veryone relies on me because I'm a good friend
X marks the spot, I love treasure hunts.
C ome follow me, my adventures are the best!
I will always be on time and willing to help!
T rying to save goals is my favourite thing to do.
E nergy is something I have a lot of, so I am always motivated.
D ad and Mom are the people I love the most.

**Toby Woodhouse (9)**
St Bartholomew's CE Primary School, Stourport-On-Severn

# Loving

**L** ots of love for friends and family.
**O** utpouring care for everyone.
**V** isiting my grannies, I love them a lot.
**I** 'm going to play with my brothers, it is my favourite.
**N** ot fighting with my brothers, I am playing!
**G** oing to the park where I spend time with the boys after school.

## Herbie Nunn (9)
St Bartholomew's CE Primary School, Stourport-On-Severn

# Dancing Queen

Release an emotion,
Dancing by the ocean,
Doing our show
The props we throw

Our mission to win the competition
Dancin' it and prancin' it
We gotta win
It won't take a min!

Gossiping away
On a Friday
"I hate school!"
"It's so cruel!"

**Olivia Augyte (10)**
St Bartholomew's CE Primary School, Stourport-On-Severn

# A Puppy Recipe

You get a cute puppy.
You need to gather a pot of love and dog food.
Stir in a dollop of love and fun so he'll play all the time!
Season with a scent of treats.
Add a pinch of loyalty and love with a little bit of good dog food.
Mix all of these together and you get Sim, the best dog in the world!

**Caelum Hill (10)**
St Bartholomew's CE Primary School, Stourport-On-Severn

# This Is Me

This is Trixie
Soft as a fluffy coat
Cute as a kitten
Loving me, making me happy
Playing all the time
Eating like a polar bear
Enjoying me throwing lightning-fast balls
Going outside all the time
This is my four-legged friend, Trixie.

**Blake Thomas (9)**
St Bartholomew's CE Primary School, Stourport-On-Severn

# The Recipe Of Bobby

First, gather a truckload of love
Sprinkle it with a bit of cuteness
Include a dash of the universe
Chuck a bucket of energy in
And you get my cat - Bobby.

**Corey James Clark (9)**
St Bartholomew's CE Primary School, Stourport-On-Severn

# A Riddle

Can you run as fast as me?
I use my hind legs to pounce
Everywhere is my hunting ground
I eat hyenas
What am I?

**Cowen Ash (9)**
St Bartholomew's CE Primary School, Stourport-On-Severn

# This Is Me

I love to dance, I love to play,
I love to do it every day!
I love the dogs, and pandas, too,
And many animals in our zoo!
I love my friends they are such fun,
I love to play with them in the sun,
My favourite sport is padel game,
And I can play it the whole day!
My favourite song is Katie's "Roar",
It is inspiring with awe,
It always makes me sing along,
I want to listen to it all day long!
And when I am bored I go to town,
To do some shopping, look around,
And after town I stroll back home,
Because it's the best place in the whole world!

**Eliana Kozliar (10)**
St Edward's Royal Free Ecumenical Middle School, Windsor

# This Is Me

I like to sing, I like to dance,
I have so many dreams all at once.
I cook, I play the piano and flute as well,
there's even more to that and I'm just about to tell...
God created me the way I wanted to be,
and even when I don't like myself at times,
I know I am surrounded by friends and family.
I actually wake up quite early instead of late,
because my mind goes in buzzes when it's a new school day.
I like to read books and let my mind carry me away,
to story land where I meet my friends, the characters,
and change the story by saying "Hey!"
It's the same when I dance and by that I mean ballet,
I feel like I can fly in an elegant way.
Sometimes, I imagine a world where there is a pink sky,
stairs made out of clouds and some kittens pop up

leaving me to stroke them until
they go back in the clouds at night.
But when it is 'bedtime' I don't go to sleep,
I hang out with my friends until it is 3.
Out of that world I am a normal school girl in year 6,
but all of that poem creates one simple word,
which is...
Me!

## Alice
St Edward's Royal Free Ecumenical Middle School, Windsor

# This Is Me!

I am happy.
I feel happy when I have chocolate.
I am like a Ferris wheel of laughter.
I am happy when I see my dog playing in the garden.
I am me.

I am loved.
I feel loved when my dad hugs me.
I am like a king being loved by the whole world.
I am loved when I make a friend.
I am me.

I am sad.
I feel sad when people are sarcastic.
I am like a feather falling into a puddle.
I am sad when people bully me.
I am me.

I am playful.
I feel playful when I am outside playing knights.
I am like a dog playing 'fetch'.

I am playful when I am on the iPad.
I am me.

## Ernest Punkenhofer-Silve (8)
St George's School, Edgbaston

# This Is Me!

To create me, you will need:

A dash of fun and excitement
A slice of cheesy pizza
A pinch of tears
A drop of happiness
A dash of a book-filled room
A drop of imagination

Put a drop of imagination in the bowl.
Now, fill the bowl with books.
Next, add a drop of happiness.
Fourth step, start stirring and, at the same time, put in the drops of tears.
Now, stop stirring and add in the cheesy pizza.
Then, add a dash of fun and excitement.
Finally, stir powerfully and you have made me.

**Emma Szlanka (7)**
St George's School, Edgbaston

# I Am Me!

I am happy.
I am happy when I play with my friends, my cousins and my dad.
I feel like Superman saving the day.
I am happy when I have free time.
I am me.

I am sad.
I felt sad when my uncle left me and went to Pakistan.
I feel like a dog with no owner.
I feel like a rock star with nobody cheering for me.
I am me.

I am playful.
I feel playful when my cousin is free to play with me.
I feel like Thor throwing the hammer at Hulk.
I am playful when I have my toys.
I am me.

## Abdullah Araf (8)
St George's School, Edgbaston

# This Is Me!

To create me, you will need:

20g of game-filled rooms
A sprinkle of speed
A dash of kindness
A little sprinkle of anger
1kg of sense
Large slices of pepperoni
Blackcurrant juice

First, pour in the game-filled room.
Add the dash of speed.
Pour in a spot of kindness.
Mix in a kilogram of sugar.
Stir in a sprinkle of anger.
Drop in a large slice of pepperoni.
Pour in and stir the blackcurrant juice.
Put in the oven for 50 minutes.

**Karanveer**
St George's School, Edgbaston

# A Recipe Poem

To create me, you will need:

A sprinkle of fun and mischief
A cup of warm tea
A pinch of naughtiness
A spoonful of sugar
A cup of candy
A bedroom full of toys

First, you will need to get a bowl and add the warm tea.
Then, sprinkle in the fun and mischief.
Next, add a pinch of naughtiness.
After that, add the spoonful of sugar.
Last but not least, add half a cup of candy.
Then, spread over the bedroom full of toys.

**Jode Lotay**
St George's School, Edgbaston

# A Recipe Poem

To create me, you will need:

A dash of disappointment
10lb of happiness and mischief
A pinch of fun
A sprinkle of excitement
A plate of dosa

First, add 10lb of happiness and mischief.
Then, mix in a book-filled bedroom.
Stir thoroughly while adding a plate of dosa.
Next, add a pinch of fun and a dash of disappointment.
Spread the mix neatly over a bug tray of happy baking paper.
Cook until glazed and fun-filled.

**Mukul Kottilil (8)**
St George's School, Edgbaston

# This Is Me!

I am happy.
I am happy when I am cuddling my dog.
I am like a big, fluffy teddy.
I am happy when my family cuddles me.
I am me.

I am loved.
I am loved when my brother plays with me.
I am like a baby being cuddled for the first time.
I am loved when my teacher says "Well done!"
I am me.

I am sad.
I feel sad when nobody lets me be their friend.
I am like a sad sloth.
I am me.

**Alicia Roberts (9)**
St George's School, Edgbaston

# A Recipe Poem

To create me, you will need:

A pinch of laughter
An iPad full of games
A library full of books
A PS4 full of charge
A group of joyful people
A handful of love

First, mix a pinch of laughter with a handful of love.
Then, add a group of joyful people.
Next, stir in 10lb of football and mischief.
After that, blend it all together with some happiness.
Finally, bake in the oven for 30 minutes.

### Mikail Iqbal (8)
St George's School, Edgbaston

# This Is Me!

Ingredients

A bedroom filled with clothes
A plate of pancakes
10lb of fast go-karts
A pinch of chocolate cake
A dash of nerves

First, put a pinch of chocolate in the bowl.
Then, mix in a plate of pancakes.
Stir in a big room of clothes.
Next, add a dash of nerves.
Finally, stir in 10lb of fast go-karts.

**Kasim Iqbal (7)**
St George's School, Edgbaston

# This Is Me!

I like to play football with my friends.
I do not like wasps, they can sting.
I like colouring because it makes me happy.
I like sleeping in on Saturdays.
I do not like tennis, because I don't know how to play.
This is me.

## Buhari
St George's School, Edgbaston

# This Is Me

**C** aring girl and super kind girl.
**A** rtist person and artist lover.
**R** oller skater person and also puppy lover.
**O** nion hater and especially pickle hater.
**L** earning girl and smart girl.
**I** 'm always getting told off at home for being naughty.
**N** ovember is the best month and so is December.
**A** m always kind and also a great helper and don't forget me, the best ball fetcher.

## Carolina Malpao (9)
St Hugh's CE Primary School, Holts

# This Is Me

I like football (that's for sure)
Cats and dogs
I love swimming
I love ice cream
Sweet eater
Love swimming
I support Man United
I'm an Oldham fan
I hate Man City
Family hugger
I like cats and dogs
Reading lover
Likes helping and likes playing with friends
Hates singing
Very jumpy.

**Josie-Lea Seddon (8)**
St Hugh's CE Primary School, Holts

# Poem About Me

**C** asper is my name
**A** nd I like playing,
**S** o much fun! Actually loads! But I don't have
**P** uppies, kittens, dogs and cats or any pets
**E** xactly, I know it is odd but please don't
**R** oast me if my poem is bad.

## Casper Marczynski (8)
St Hugh's CE Primary School, Holts

# This Is Me

F orests are dark
A pples are so juicy and green
R aining is not good because I cannot play outside
I 'm a good friend
Y ucky mud is brown
A pricots are my fav fruit
H ide-and-seek is my fav game.

**Fariyah Farooq (8)**
St Hugh's CE Primary School, Holts

# All About Me

I like football
I play for a team.
I like cuddling my dog.
I love art.
I like playing with my friends.
My dog is so fast.
I love my family.
I love my baby cousins,
I like swimming.
I like cats.
I like birds.

## Macie-Dee Seddon (8)
St Hugh's CE Primary School, Holts

# My Rap Poem

I am a sporty kid
I like football
I am fan
I like jumping up and down
And making my mum proud
I am a good gymnast and actor
I care for my friends and family
I am nice some days but some days I am angry
I speak French.

**Christopher Allen (9)**
St Hugh's CE Primary School, Holts

# I Love Me

I love me.
I like painting art.
My bearded dragon is my best pet.
I love football, it is my favourite game.
My game that I like is bulldog.
I love swimming, it's my favourite lesson
My game is dodgeball.

**Kyron Peers (9)**
St Hugh's CE Primary School, Holts

# Rap About Me

I am as fast as a flash
I love to eat and sleep
Not an early riser and a slow walker
Fast sleeper, good catcher
Big fan of football
Good helper
Good mind
A big fan of dodgeball
And I like to cook.

**Reis Matoshi (9)**
St Hugh's CE Primary School, Holts

# This Is Me

Hello my name is Ellis,
And I like football,
I am a Man United lover,
And a superstar goalkeeper,
My best friend is Reis,
And I love family,
I play for Springhead,
And I am a generous guy!

**Ellis Musoni (8)**
St Hugh's CE Primary School, Holts

# Rap About Me

Yo my name is Abigail,
I like football that's for sure!
I'm good at art and I'm super smart,
I'm sweet and sour with lots of power!
I eat sweets non-stop, chocolate and lollipops!

## Abigail Aina (8)
St Hugh's CE Primary School, Holts

# My Favourite Sport

I use my legs but also my arms
I move but it's quite easy
I go to it in school, it's really fun
It is not dance but also not PE
If there's no water I can not do it
What is it?

**Lexi Taylor (9)**
St Hugh's CE Primary School, Holts

# This Is Me

**M** y favourite colour is red.
**I** love playing on monkey bars.
**K** aney is my best friend
**A** fter school I play with my friends Aisha and Ayat.

## Mika Ross (9)
St Hugh's CE Primary School, Holts

# This Is Me

**B** eautiful lover
**Y** ou will not see me play football
**R** unning very fast
**O** bvious I love math
**N** obody loves my dog like me.

## Byron Pember (8)
St Hugh's CE Primary School, Holts

# All About Me

I am tall
I like cooking
I like swimming.
Dogs are my favourite.
I like art
I like pasta.
I like dodgeball
I like cats.

**Jakub Gryszka (9)**
St Hugh's CE Primary School, Holts

# This Is Me

*A kennings poem*

Winter needer.
Tuna hater.
Ice cream eater.
Roblox player.
Book enjoyer.
Dog lover.
Flower smeller.
Family wanter.

## Daniel Allen (8)
St Hugh's CE Primary School, Holts

# This Is Me

**N** ot a football fan
**A** nts hater
**O** range eater
**M** ega sleeper
**I** am a gymnastic fan.

## Naomi Kendra Ndlovu (8)
St Hugh's CE Primary School, Holts

# Sea Swimming

When I am feeling low,
Off to the beach I go,
Running through the sand to the sea,
This is where I can finally be me!

The first cold wave splashing in my face,
Sea salt spraying all over the place,
I kick my legs, arms to the sky,
The sea makes me feel like I can fly.

Small fish swimming by,
Seaweed brushing past my thigh,
Distant boats under the sun's rays,
I always dream that I could be on one some day,

Time flown past,
I splash my last,
Out I get soaking wet,
How beautiful it is to watch the sun set.

## Keeva Gilchrist (11)
St Mary's Primary School Dunsford, Ardglass

# This Is Me

T umbling and flipping is a hobby that I like to do.
H andstands and cartwheels are very fun to me.
I reland is one of my favourite countries and also Scotland.
S nakes are very cool and I like their long tongues.

I n the summer, on the beach, I like to play in the water.
S carlet is one of my favourite colours.

M arshmallows and fruit are very tasty and delicious.
E verything I do, I try to enjoy it and do it as best I can.

## Eva Mae Magee (8)
St Mary's Primary School Dunsford, Ardglass

# This Is Me

**T** errific horse rider, I am amazing at it.
**H** and ball player through and through.
**I** nterested in American football.
**S** imply adores Harry Potter, I love it!

**I** love my family so so much!
**S** uper good with animals, I love all animals!

**M** y all-time favourite food is mash and gravy.
**E** xcellent with horses, I love them so much and I think they love me too!

## Isabelle Burns (10)
St Mary's Primary School Dunsford, Ardglass

# This Is Me

**T** he favourite thing I like to do is gymnastics.
**H** ello, my name is Nicole.
**I** like to play with my friends.
**S** ometimes I don't like to do my homework.

**I** like monkeys because they are energetic like me.
**S** ome day I will win first in a gymnastics competition.

**M** y favourite colour is yellow.
**E** veryone in my family supports me for what I love.

## Nicole Karbauske (8)
St Mary's Primary School Dunsford, Ardglass

# This Is Me

**T** he thing I love doing most is hanging on the monkey bars.
**H** elping others makes me feel very happy.
**I** love my family, they make me feel safe and happy.
**S** wimming is the best.

**I** like playing Roblox, it is a fun game to play.
**S** picy food is what I like most.

**M** aths is something I do not like.
**E** ach day I still try my best!

## Lottie Smyth (8)
St Mary's Primary School Dunsford, Ardglass

# This Is Me

T his is me, David Kelly
H aving fun at home and school
I n the classroom doing work
S itting and playing at lunchtime too.

I n the morning, it's time to work
S itting next to my friends, wanting to learn.

M r Fitzpatrick helps us a lot
E ven my friends, we learn what we're taught.

**David Kelly (10)**
St Mary's Primary School Dunsford, Ardglass

# This Is Me

**T** he farm is where I like to be.
**H** arry is my name.
**I** like being with my family.
**S** chool is where I meet my friends.

**I** sla and Charlie are my sister and brother.
**S** wimming is one of my favourite sports.

**M** y mum makes very nice food.
**E** very day my friends make me happy.

## Harry Gilchrist (9)
St Mary's Primary School Dunsford, Ardglass

# This Is Me

T he world's funniest kid.
H appy all the time.
I love playing gorilla tag.
S uper smart at English and maths.

I love my dog, my cat, my rabbit and my chickens.
S uper at art and drawing.

M y family loves me and my sister.
E ats all different food and records it.

**Ollie Mc Mullan (9)**
St Mary's Primary School Dunsford, Ardglass

# A Recipe For Me

**T** en cups of trust.
**H** alf a spoonful of jokes.
**I** n a bowl and mix together.
**S** poon in some laughs.

**I** n the bowl and bake.
**S** hake well, add some arts, crafts and football skills.

**M** aybe a little bit of love and what do you have?
**E** njoying a recipe to describe me.

## Rossa Curran (8)
St Mary's Primary School Dunsford, Ardglass

# This Is Me

**T** he best thing in the world is football.
**H** arry is my best friend.
**I** love playing Gaelic.
**S** coring is the best.

**I** love doing maths.
**S** ums are so easy.

**M** y granny makes the best food.
**E** llie my dog is the best dog I have because she does not shed.

## Dara Gilchrist (8)
St Mary's Primary School Dunsford, Ardglass

# This Is Me

**T** his is me, Callum
**H** elpful and kind
**I** like to play football and my Xbox
**S** hare my toys and sweets

**I** like to play football
**S** ocialise with my friends

**M** unch on vegetables and salad
**E** njoying family time with my dog.

## Callum Moreland (9)
St Mary's Primary School Dunsford, Ardglass

# This Is Me

T he thing I like to do is doodle.
H appy and kind.
I s loving and caring.
S ays great things to people.

I s always happy.
S ays good things to friends.

M y name is Michelle.
E asy to play with friends.

**Michelle Sniuke (8)**
St Mary's Primary School Dunsford, Ardglass

# This Is Me

**T** ired of homework
**H** aving fun with my friends
**I** love playing Fortnite
**S** uper kind

**I** love playing Roblox
**S** uper fun

**M** y favourite sport is tennis
**E** ager to have fun.

## Callum Mc Ilmail (9)
St Mary's Primary School Dunsford, Ardglass

# This Is Me

I am not like my naughty cat
I like going on train rides but I'm not a steam train
I love going to the cinema but I am not popcorn and sweets
I like ants but I am not an insect
I like movies but I am not a movie or a film
I like the beach but I am not a crab or a fish
I like poems, that's why I'm writing a 'This Is Me' poem
I like flying like a parachute
I like digging like a coal miner
I like swinging but I am not a monkey
I know fire is hot like the sun
I love running but I can't run like Sonic
I love planets but I am not the solar system
I like plants but I'm not a leaf
I like monster trucks they are fun to play with
I love video games but I'm not a video gamer.
This is me.

**Jack Bell (6)**
St Michael's RC Primary School, East Ham

# Family

  **F**  avourite people in the world are my family members
  **A**  lways I like to play and spend time in my home,
  **M**  y favourite food is my mum's delicious traditional food,
  **I**  love my family and friends so much,
  **L**  ove and caring are symbols of my family
  **Y**  ellow and sky blue are my favourite colours.

I love my family so much,
Always I want to see my family be happy,
I don't like to see sad in my family's face,
I don't like to see my baby crying
And also I don't like raw foods,
Always thank you God gives me such a blessed family
Please protect and bless me my family
I love you so much my family
Thank God in our all blessings.

### Nohan Jose (6)
St Michael's RC Primary School, East Ham

# Games And Cruz

I am as strong as my dad
I can run faster than my dad
I can jump higher than my mum
My favourite pets are my dogs and cats
I eat faster but I am not pasta
I eat apple but I am not an apple tree
My favourite toy is a Sonic toy.
I can beat people at football but
I'm not that good at basketball.
My friends are fast when playing tag
I can run fast but my friends are faster
Tag is my favourite game. I like it.
When I laugh I get weak.
Everything is hard and difficult
My second best game is Ninjago
My next best game is Minecraft.
My third best game is Mario.
My fourth best game is Hero Academy.

**Cruz Vickery (6)**
St Michael's RC Primary School, East Ham

# This Is Me

I like to do art and I will be famous one day
I like to read and I will be an author one day
I like Google Classroom and I will be a teacher one day
I like to eat orange, I will never be an orange one day
I like to watch TV, I will be on it one day

I like bananas because it is friends with orange
I like babies because they are little with tiny toes
I like cats because they have long whiskers
I like dogs because they talk with a woof woof
I like music because it makes me dance
I like Reading Eggs. It makes me smarter with words.

## Stephanie Bartha (6)
St Michael's RC Primary School, East Ham

# This Is Me

My name is Mayan and I like school
I am always folding things but I am not a folder
I love scooting and not driving in a car
I hate getting punched but I am not a puncher
I hate getting pushed but I am not a pusher
I love playtime and I love RE at school
I hate my sister pranking on me
I like watching parachutes but I don't like heights
I like pranking my mum and dad and I love my family
I love bananas, they are cool to eat
I love eating bananas in the aeroplane
Mayan loves and Mayan likes everything.

## Mayan Fagan (6)
St Michael's RC Primary School, East Ham

# My Likes

I am Szofi
I love my mum, I am her daughter.
I love ice cream but I am not ice.
I love dancing but I am not a dancer.
I love candy but I am not a lollipop
I love school but I am not a teacher
I love my mum but I am not a mum
I love adventures but I am not a mountain
I love fur but I am not a cat
I love jumping but I am not a bunny
I love cutting but I am not a woodcutter.
I love Szofi and Szofi loves me.

## Szofi Gal (6)
St Michael's RC Primary School, East Ham

# This Is Janella

I like honey but I am not a bear.
I like dancing but I am not a ballerina.
I like jumping but I am not a kangaroo.
I wish I could dig with paws like a dog.
I am strong but not like my sister.
I like scaring people but I am not a ghost.
I like painting but I am not an artist.
I like to meow, pretending to be a cat.
I like tiny people but I am not a baby.
I am just me, a girl called Janella.

**Janella Budu-Aggrey (6)**
St Michael's RC Primary School, East Ham

# Ayva The Lover

I love IT but I am not a computer.
I love singing but I am not a singer
I love running but I am not a lion
I love cleaning but I am not a cleaner
I love reading but I am not a book.
I love bananas but I am not a monkey
I love science but I am not a scientist
I love baking with Mum but I am not a baker
I love sleeping when the clouds are heavy with rain.
Ayva loves almost everything.

## Ayva-Oakly Annan-Mathieu (6)
St Michael's RC Primary School, East Ham

# Unicorn Me

I like going to the park to look for unicorns
I like eating honey with my unicorns
I like apples but I am not an apple tree
I like unicorns
I would like to feed unicorns ice cream
I would like to feed unicorns ice cream in the moonlight
I would like to feel unicorns ice cream on the green grass
I would like to feed unicorns on top of the green apple trees
I like unicorns.

## Skylar Delisser (7)
St Michael's RC Primary School, East Ham

# Elkanah Likes Things

I am Elkanah
I like furry things but I am not a cat.
I like to sleep but I am not a sofa bed
I am Elkanah and I know Claudia Jones
I learnt about her in Black History Month
She made the Notting Hill Carnival
I like honey but I am not a bee
I would like to live in a castle like a queen
Not a queen bee but a real queen
I like all colours but I am not a rainbow.

**Elkhanah Theresa Shijanjose (6)**
St Michael's RC Primary School, East Ham

# Inspire Me

**I** ncluding people in all my playground games
**N** otifications from my Google Classroom for my homework
**S** hine as bright as the yellow sun, that's me.
**P** ing pong is my favourite game
**I** like Reading Eggs for good learning.
**R** evolution happens sometimes in my learning.
**E** verything I do with my teacher inspires me.

## Anaiah Grace Oduwole (7)
St Michael's RC Primary School, East Ham

# I'm Happy

I'm loud but I am not a lion
I'm fast but I am not a cheetah
I'm sneaky but I am not a fox
I'm wiggly but I am not a worm
I'm fun and not boring
I'm brown but not a horse
I'm big but I am not an elephant
I'm smart and I have great ideas
I'm kind, kind, kind, so kind.

**Ishmael Menchaca (6)**
St Michael's RC Primary School, East Ham

# Aeroplanes Are Me

Aeroplanes like me and I like aeroplanes
If I could fly as fast as an aeroplane
If I could have long wings like an aeroplane
If I go up in the cool air like an aeroplane
If I had a pointy nose like an aeroplane
If I could roar like an aeroplane
If I could be an aeroplane
I would be a happy aeroplane, living in an aeroplane.

## Evaan Joharsingh (6)
St Michael's RC Primary School, East Ham

# This Is Me

**T** hick curly hair and dimples in my cheeks
**H** appy, cheeky, friendly me.
**I** like playing with Lego
**S** hooting stars and birthdays.

**I** love singing and swimming
**S** lime-making is fun and messy

**M** um and I playing.
**E** lla is my sister, she is my favourite person.

## Joseph Ogarro (7)
St Michael's RC Primary School, East Ham

# I Am River

I like yellow
It's a bright colour
I love maths
I add my tens and ones
I love music
I like forte and piano sounds
I love spelling
I learned phonics for spellings.
I love writing
I love lemons
I love reading
I love IT
I love to try my best in maths
I like being good.

## River Carter (6)
St Michael's RC Primary School, East Ham

# Pet School

**S** quirrels, I love to feed them nuts
**C** ats are my favourite pets with whiskers
**H** orses are my second best pet with a mane
**O** tters are my favourite animals that live in water
**O** ranges are just a fruit I like. Horses like them too.
**L** aughing makes me happy, happy with my pet.

## Stacey Wu (7)
St Michael's RC Primary School, East Ham

# Yellow Blue

I like the blue-yellow sky
I like the blue-yellow sides
I like my blue-yellow class
I like my blue-yellow house
I like my blue-yellow friends
And my blue-yellow clothes
Everything about me is blue or yellow.
I see everything as blue and yellow.
What colours do you see?

**Sarthak Pathak (6)**
St Michael's RC Primary School, East Ham

# I Like Pink

I like pink
I like running in pink
I like playing in pink
I like maths when the numbers are pink
I like colours that are so pink
I like art better whenever it's pink
I have a white school PE kit but not pink
Only if my school PE kit was pink
That would be great!

**Riya Jerry (6)**
St Michael's RC Primary School, East Ham

# This Is Me

I like red
It sounds like bread
I like water
It sounds like butter
I like Messi
He is a famous football player
I like spicy chicken
Cooked in our kitchen
I love red ice lollies
I love red strawberries
I love pepper
I love red but I am not a colour.

**Nadal Maxwell (6)**
St Michael's RC Primary School, East Ham

# This Is Me

I like to jump but I am not a kangaroo
I like being hot but I am not an oven
I like eating oranges but my skin isn't orange
What else do I like?
Oh! I like running, jumping and dancing
I like reading stories
I like so many things
I cannot think of all of them now.

**Natchatrah Sivamathan**
St Michael's RC Primary School, East Ham

# Hiding

**H** orses are my best friend
**I** can hide underneath their fluffy tail
**D** ogs are my favourite animals
**I** can't hide behind their cold button nose
**N** ot all animals are big enough to hide me.
**G** rasshoppers are just too small.

**Anastasia Berdaga-Roabis (6)**
St Michael's RC Primary School, East Ham

# Hello Green

I love green trees
I love green bananas
I taste green lime
Yuk! Yuk! Yuk!
I like green peas
I like green pies
I don't know why!
I love green stories
About our green planet
I am in the green zone
I'm happy, happy, green happy.

**Isaac Wilson (7)**
St Michael's RC Primary School, East Ham

# This Is Me

My name is Neymar
I love to play with my friends
I love to play with my neighbours
I like my new toys
I like to go to the park to play on the swings
I love to go to the cinemas to watch movies
I like to go to church to pray to God.

## Neymar Maxwell (6)
St Michael's RC Primary School, East Ham

# This Is Poppy

I love dogs but I'm not one
I love cats but I'm not one.
I love teachers because they teach me maths.
I love Freddie, my cousin and
I love Ronnie, too.
I love games.
I am Poppy
I love red!
Yes, yes, yes.

**Poppy O'Connell (6)**
St Michael's RC Primary School, East Ham

# Rabbit And I

Rabbit
Hello rabbit
I love rabbit
I love white rabbit
Do you?
When I am in the wild
I look for white rabbits
Look at me
I found a white rabbit
It's wiggly.

**Cianna Green**
St Michael's RC Primary School, East Ham

# This Is Me

Hi my name is Rocco and I have a dream to complete...
When I play football I'm like the wind, stealthy, swift and strong.
I sneak up on you when you're not expecting it.
When I'm on my mountain bike I feel free like a horse
Running down a majestic beach with the sun setting behind me.
I feel lost without my bike
It's like I'm trying to walk down an escalator that's going up.

**Rocco Hulcup (11)**
Stonesfield Primary School, Stonesfield

# My Favourite Place!

**B** oats sailing on the wonderful sea.
**E** veryone running into the water in excitement.
**A** seagull stealing people's food and being cheeky.
**C** runch goes my ice cream, I enjoy a cold treat.
**H** appy feelings on the beach and having a good time.

## Freya Harris (10)
Stonesfield Primary School, Stonesfield

# My Favourite Place

**B** alls rolling down the aisles.
**O** h I love getting strikes.
**W** ins are my favourite.
**L** arge balls are the heaviest.
**I** 'm not amazing but I try.
**N** ice seats plotted down.
**G** oing to go bowling at every opportunity.

**James Hunt (10)**
Stonesfield Primary School, Stonesfield

# Isaac S.M.

**I** nterested in almost everything
**S** ports aren't my thing
**A** mazing at drawing and writing
**A** xolotl lover
**C** reative and smart

**S** illy video game player

**M** aster at making people laugh.

## Isaac Smyth-Medina (11)
Stonesfield Primary School, Stonesfield

# Sports

**S** uper speedy like a flash
**P** ast the finishing line in first place
**O** ne of the best in hockey
**R** eally just incredible on the slopes
**T** he king of skiing
**S** uper fun and competitive.

## Abel Stuart (10)
Stonesfield Primary School, Stonesfield

# This Is Me

**L** oving my computers
**E** very day eats sweets
**L** oves my family
**A** lways helps people
**N** ever let anyone down before
**D** oes any tasks from teachers or parents.

**Leland Edwards (10)**
Stonesfield Primary School, Stonesfield

# YOUNG WRITERS INFORMATION

We hope you have enjoyed reading this book – and that you will continue to in the coming years.

If you're the parent or family member of an enthusiastic poet or story writer, do visit our website www.youngwriters.co.uk/subscribe and sign up to receive news, competitions, writing challenges and tips, activities and much, much more! There's lots to keep budding writers motivated!

If you would like to order further copies of this book, or any of our other titles, then please give us a call or order via your online account.

Young Writers
Remus House
Coltsfoot Drive
Peterborough
PE2 9BF
(01733) 890066
info@youngwriters.co.uk

Join in the conversation!
Tips, news, giveaways and much more!

 YoungWritersUK    YoungWritersCW    youngwriterscw

Scan me to watch the This Is Me video!